Learn GERMAN Through

Cinderella

Book Design & Production: Slangman Kids (a division of Slangman Inc. and Slangman Publishing)

Copy Editor: Julie Bobrick
Illustrated by: "Migs!" Sandoval
Translators: Teut Deese & Petra Wirth
Proofreader: Kai Cofer

Copyright © 2006 by David Burke

Published by: Slangman Kids (a division of Slangman Inc. and Slangman Publishing) 12206 Hillslope Street, Studio City, CA 91604 •USA • Toll Free Telephone from USA: 1-877-SLANGMAN (1-877-752-6462) • From outside the USA: 1-818-SLANGMAN (1-818-752-6462) • Worldwide Fax 1-413-647-1589 • Email: info@slangman.com • Website: www.slangman.com

"Migs!" Sandoval
✳ our illustrator ✳

Miguel *"Migs!"* Sandoval has been drawing cartoons since the age of 6 and has worked on numerous national commercials and movies as a sculptor, model builder, and illustrator. He was born in Los Angeles and was raised in a bilingual household, speaking English and Spanish. He currently lives in San Francisco where he is working on his new comic book series!

ISBN10: 1891888-765
ISBN13: 978189888-762
Printed in the U.S.A.

10 9 8 7 6 5 4 3 2 1

Order Form

Preview chapters & shop online!

www.slangman.com

SHIP TO: _____

_____

_____

_____

Contact/Phone/Email: _____

SHIPPING

Domestic Orders

SURFACE MAIL
(Delivery time 5-7 business days).
Add $5 shipping/handling for the first item, $1.50 for each additional item.

RUSH SERVICE
Available at extra charge. Contact us for details.

International Orders

SURFACE MAIL
(Delivery time 6-8 weeks).
Add $6 shipping/handling for the first item, $2 for each additional item. Note that shipping to some countries may be more expensive. Contact us for details.

AIRMAIL (approx. 3-5 business days)
Available at extra charge. Contact us for details.

Method of Payment (Check one):

☐ Personal Check or Money Order
(Must be in U.S. funds and drawn on a U.S. bank.)

☐ VISA ☐ Master Card ☐ Discover ☐ American Express ☐ JCB

Credit Card Number

☐ Signature   ☐ ☐ ☐ Expiration Date

QTY	ISBN-13	TITLE	PRICE	LEVEL	TOTAL COST
English to CHINESE (Mandarin)					
	9781891888-793	Cinderella	$14.95	1	
	9781891888-854	Goldilocks	$14.95	2	
	9781891888-915	Beauty and the Beast	$14.95	3	
English to FRENCH					
	9781891888-755	Cinderella	$14.95	1	
	9781891888-816	Goldilocks	$14.95	2	
	9781891888-878	Beauty and the Beast	$14.95	3	
English to GERMAN					
	9781891888-762	Cinderella	$14.95	1	
	9781891888-830	Goldilocks	$14.95	2	
	9781891888-885	Beauty and the Beast	$14.95	3	
English to HEBREW					
	9781891888-922	Cinderella	$14.95	1	
	9781891888-939	Goldilocks	$14.95	2	
	9781891888-946	Beauty and the Beast	$14.95	3	
English to ITALIAN					
	9781891888-779	Cinderella	$14.95	1	
	9781891888-823	Goldilocks	$14.95	2	
	9781891888-892	Beauty and the Beast	$14.95	3	
English to JAPANESE					
	9781891888-786	Cinderella	$14.95	1	
	9781891888-847	Goldilocks	$14.95	2	
	9781891888-908	Beauty and the Beast	$14.95	3	
English to SPANISH					
	9781891888-748	Cinderella	$14.95	1	
	9781891888-809	Goldilocks	$14.95	2	
	9781891888-861	Beauty and the Beast	$14.95	3	
Japanese to ENGLISH 絵本で えいご を学ぼう					
	9781891888-038	Cinderella	$14.95	1	
	9781891888-045	Goldilocks	$14.95	2	
	9781891888-052	Beauty and the Beast	$14.95	3	
Korean to ENGLISH 동화를 통한 ENGLISH 배우기					
	9781891888-076	Cinderella	$14.95	1	
	9781891888-106	Goldilocks	$14.95	2	
	9781891888-113	Beauty and the Beast	$14.95	3	
Spanish to ENGLISH Aprende INGLÉS con cuentos de hadas					
	9781891888-953	Cinderella	$14.95	1	
	9781891888-960	Goldilocks	$14.95	2	
	9781891888-977	Beauty and the Beast	$14.95	3	

Total for Merchandise _____

Sales Tax *(California residents only add applicable sales tax)* _____

Shipping *(See left)* _____

ORDER GRAND TOTAL _____

Prices subject to change

SLANGMAN® KIDS

(a division of Slangman Publishing)

** TO PLACE AN ORDER - CALL, FAX, OR EMAIL: **

Phone: 1-818-752-6462 • Fax: 1-413-647-1589
Email: info@slangman.com • Web: www.slangman.com
12206 Hillslope Street • Studio City, CA 91604

(FORM 071606)

Dedication

The entire "Foreign Language Through Fairy Tales" series is dedicated to all the children of the world.

It is through their understanding, appreciation, and celebration of our differences that the world will become a better and safer place for us all.

A few things to remember...

- In this fairy tale, you'll notice that some of the German words have a new letter of the alphabet. It's the letter "ß" which looks a lot like our letter "B," but it's not! It's called an "eszett" which is used to represent "ss." For example:

    foot = **Fuss**, but it's always written as **Fuß**.
    big = **gross**, but it's always written as **groß**.

- You'll notice that in German, all nouns (those words that represent a person, place, or thing) begin with an uppercase letter. That's because in German, ALL nouns are written this way! For example:

    girl = **Mädchen** • **house** = **Haus** • **party** = **Fest** • **prince** = **Prinz**

1

Mädchen ←

hübsch ←

Haus ←

Once upon a time, there lived a poor [girl] named Cinderella who was very [pretty]. The **Mädchen**, who was very **hübsch**, lived in a small [house] with her stepmother and two

stepsisters. At times it was difficult for the poor **Mädchen** to live in such a small **Haus** with her stepmother and stepsisters. Why? Because they were

3

böse ← jealous that she was so **hübsch** which is why her stepmother was extra mean to her. But the poor **Mädchen** never complained about living in a small

Haus with her stepmother, who was very **böse**, and stepsisters, even though they forced her to do all the work in the entire **Haus** day in and day out!

5

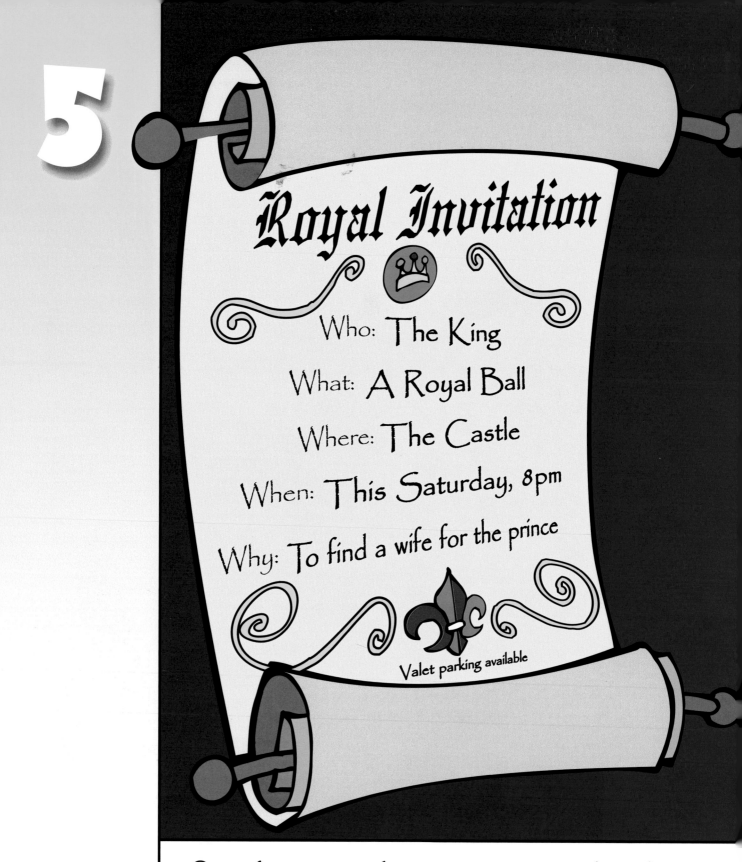

Royal Invitation

Who: The King

What: A Royal Ball

Where: The Castle

When: This Saturday, 8pm

Why: To find a wife for the prince

Valet parking available

One day, a royal invitation arrived at the **Haus** of the poor **Mädchen**. The king was throwing a party for the prince. And the **Fest** was going to be big. The **Fest**

Fest ←

groß ←

6

was going to be *very* **groß**! The prince was
handsome, not only **stattlich**, but kind.
And every **Mädchen** in the land was invited
to the **Fest** so that he could choose a wife.

→ **stattlich**

→ **Frau**

7

Prinz

The king and queen also hoped the (prince) would find a **Frau** who was truly **hübsch** both inside and out. The **Prinz** was very excited about his royal **Fest**!

The night of the **Fest** for the **Prinz** arrived but Cinderella was very ⌐sad⌐. Her step-mother was so **böse**, she wouldn't let her leave the **Haus** to go to the **Fest**!

traurig

9

She was so **traurig**, she started to cry. She was the only **Mädchen** not allowed to leave her **Haus** and get the chance to meet the **Prinz** at the **Fest** and become his **Frau**.

Suddenly a voice from behind her said, "My dear, I'm your fairy godmother and you'll be able to go to the **Fest** of the **Prinz** and... you'll be wearing an elegant dress!"

Kleid

Danke ←

And with a wave of her wand, Cinderella was now wearing the most elegant **Kleid** imaginable. "Thank you! **Danke**!" exclaimed Cinderella. She was now a

Mädchen who was truly **hübsch**, wearing an elegant **Kleid**, and eager to leave her **Haus** to meet the **Prinz** at the **Fest**, and maybe, just maybe become his **Frau**.

Moment ←

Mitternacht ←

"One [moment]!" the fairy godmother added. "Make sure to leave the **Fest** by [midnight] because your **Kleid** will change back to the way it was!"

14

Cinderella thought for a **Moment** and then said, "I'll remember to leave before **Mitternacht**." So, the **Mädchen**, who was very **hübsch**, left for the **Fest**. She

15

glücklich ←

was no longer **traurig**, but very happy to be meeting the **Prinz**. As she got out of her carriage, she could hear the **Fest** and indeed it was **groß**! Cinderella walked in

16

and wasn't too **glücklich** to see more than
one **Mädchen** waiting to meet the **Prinz**.
But after a **Moment**, she calmed down and
was ready to meet the **Prinz** face to face.

17

verliebt

And indeed he was very **stattlich**! She couldn't believe her eyes! And clearly the **Prinz** was in love at the sight of a **Mädchen** who was so **hübsch**!

"**Danke** very much for inviting me to your **Fest**" said Cinderella. "You're welcome" responded the **Prinz**. Cinderella and the **Prinz**

Gern geschehen

danced and danced for hours, until the stroke of **Mitternacht** was finally upon them which the **Mädchen** had completely forgotten about! And poof! Her **Kleid** vanished!

"Goodbye!" shouted Cinderella. "**Auf Wiedersehen**! And **danke** for inviting me!"

"**Gern geschehen**," responded the **Prinz**. And Cinderella ran back to her **Haus**.

Auf Wiedersehen

21

Schuh ← The only thing she left behind was a glass shoe. The **Prinz** was extremely **traurig** and went from town to town looking for a **Mädchen** whose

Fuß

foot would fit the glass **Schuh**.
After days of eliminating **Mädchen**
after **Mädchen**, the **Prinz** was
more **traurig** than ever, but he

had one more **Haus** to visit. The **böse** stepmother and stepsisters ran out to try on the glass **Schuh** but it was no use. He still couldn't find a **Fuß** to match the **Schuh**!

The **Prinz** was **traurig** and about to give up, but at that very **Moment**, he spotted Cinderella. There was something very special about her, aside from being so **hübsch**.

He just had to see if her **Fuß** was the one that could fit the glass **Schuh**. He knelt down in front of the **Mädchen** and slid the **Schuh** on her **Fuß**.

And her **Fuß** did fit the glass **Schuh** perfectly! Suddenly in a puff of smoke, Cinderella's fairy godmother reappeared and changed her back into the same

Mädchen in the elegant **Kleid** the **Prinz**
had met at his **Fest**. The **Prinz** was now
more **verliebt** than ever! And Cinderella was
especially **glücklich** that she lost her glass

Schuh at the **Fest** or the **Prinz** may never have found her – a **Mädchen** as **hübsch** on the inside as on the out! Soon, she became his **Frau** at a wedding that was far from

29

small. It was truly **groß**! She was so very **glücklich**! Cinderella would never, ever be **traurig** again. And the **Prinz** and Cinderella lived in the castle happily ever after.